MW00984040

'Kate Bolton Bonnici's *A True & Just Record* movingly demonstrates poetry's capacity to forge critical and philosophical dialogue across time and space. Deploying the dialogic rhetoric of stichomythia as a method of both reading and writing, Bonnici stages a conversation among sixteenth- and seventeenth-century plays, poems, and pamphlets; classical and contemporary poetry, criticism, and theory; and her own poetic meditations on memory and loss. The result is a daring and gorgeous poetic conversation that insists on the centrality of form and sound to both personal narrative and scholarly analysis.'

— Melissa E. Sanchez, Donald T. Regan Professor, University of Pennsylvania

'Witch as spell, curse, praise, eulogy, recovery, incantation, archival raid and save, library as cathedral and books as catechism—as befits poetry as anarchic art, in Kate Bolton Bonnici's hands the sacred is barbaric and the profane is holy. The link between the personal and autobiographical and the social and (inter)national is plaited with strands of song, poetry forms, and ledgers of profit weighed against loss. Bonnici's witches are revolutionary figures she links to family history, her grandmothers in particular, to show us how history is made flesh. She brings the archive to life and recovers lives otherwise lost as fragmentary entries. The way Bonnici grows these bits and pieces into cogent arguments and testimonies, philosophical treatises and affective insights, makes it easy to admire her craft and craftiness, her sly ease among the age-old and complexity of the archive, her care and grace as she handles and arranges dismissive facts about women destroyed by bigotry. The title, borrowed from a record of female persecution, is all but true and just until Bonnici's reckoning. She imagines truth and justice into the lives of her women and memorialises her grandmothers, the best poetry in coalition with an awareness of women who shape our personal and public histories. A wicked and wise achievement.'

— Fred D'Aguiar, author of *Letters to America* and *For the Unnamed*

'In her poem "Echo," Kate Bolton Bonnici quotes John Webster's macabre 1613 masterpiece *The Duchess of Malfi*: "I will not talk with thee / For thou art a dead thing." Yet it is Bonnici's profound project in *A True & Just Record* to talk with the dead—and by *with*, I mean not *at* but rather *alongside*, or *as in harmony*. Bonnici describes her imaginative engagement with the language and the thinking of archival texts as "immersive marginalia," an approach that allows her to expand, subvert, affirm, and reimagine enduring questions about gender, authority, and selfhood. Bonnici's collection reveals that, far from being remote and unapproachable, centuries-old writings remain vibrantly relevant to our own historical moment. Her deeply humane book seeks quickening rediscoveries, her poems on each new page reaching to build new and generative connections across times and selves: "And where shall we meet? And when?"'

— Kimberly Johnson, author of *Fatal*

'This incredibly insightful investigation of sensational witch trial pamphlets, rendered richly with *witch stichomythia*, is a communion of conversation deeply engaging historical and present poet discourse. Delightfully provocative lines bring fold and unfold of conjure and inquisition treatise. Here, a multitude of stellar engagements delve spiritedly into what sonic and visual presences may be made of form, utterance, accusation, exchange, and page on the troubled edge of devilish societal inquisition with interplay delivering euphony, cacophony—brilliance—in incantatory verse-play feat. Bring on the prizes, this poetry is delicious!'

— Allison Adelle Hedge Coke, author of *Look at This Blue*

A True & Just Record

Beyond Criticism Editions explores the new paths that criticism might take in the 21st century.

We encourage any kind of formal adventure: analytical, aphoristic, archival, autobiographical, citational, confessional, descriptive, dialogical, dramatic, fantastical, fictive, graphic, historical, imaginative, ironical, metaphysical, miscellaneous, mythical, palimpsestic, parasitical, philosophical, poetical, polemical, political, probational, riddling, theological, theoretical, ventriloquial.

Our only criterion is that it *discovers*.

The series is curated by Katharine Craik (Oxford Brookes University) and Simon Palfrey (Oxford University)

A True & Just Record

by Kate Bolton Bonnici

BOILER HOUSE PRESS

Beyond Criticism Editions

Contents

for my grandmothers

Fyrst she learned this arte of witchcraft at the age of
.xii. yeres of hyr grandmother whose nam was mother
Eue of Hatfyelde Peuerell disseased.

—*attributed to the examination & confession
of Elizabeth Frauncis, 1566*

Witch Stichomythia: Chances, Changes, & Strange Shapes

At the beginning of writing, there is a loss.
—Michel de Certeau, "The Unnamable"

Late March 2020. I tried over the phone to help my grandmother—97, already living alone, and now entirely isolated due to COVID-19 restrictions—figure out how to operate a laptop computer so that she could send emails and read the news online. Meanwhile in my own reading, I toggled between doomscrolling hyper-current headlines and researching English blackletter pamphlets from the 16th and 17th centuries. Some of the latter fittingly concerned plague, such as the remarkable pamphlet attributed to Thomas Dekker—*The Wonderfull yeare. 1603. Wherein is shewed the picture of London, lying sicke of the Plague.* Through prose and poetry, *The Wonderfull yeare* navigates that earlier *mirabilis annus*, as Dekker calls it, ranging from Queen Elizabeth's death to the onslaught of widespread illness, by "tell[ing] only of the chances, changes, and strange shapes that this Protean Climactericall yeare hath metamorphosed himselfe into."

Another contemporary and crucial genre of pamphlets sought to capitalize on the salacious dramas of ongoing witch trials. From the earliest extant version—*The Examination and Confession of certaine Wytches at Chensforde in the Countie of Essex, before the Quenes maiesties Judges, the xxvi. daye of July. ANNO. 1566*—scolding pamphleteers (and chroniclers) retold and sold narratives of alleged village *maleficia* emerging from the thick of sickness, violence, vulnerability, storytelling traditions, economic and political upheaval, and fear of the other. Terribly relevant reading.

Reading sometimes turns to writing when one wants communion. For writing begins, as Michel de Certeau explains, in loss. This loss lies not only in the impossible distance between presence and sign. Writing begins in want, which means both lack and desire. Writing into the want of and for communion (with far-away family, long-ago literatures, past and present scholarship) necessitates chances, changes, strange shapes.

The poems stitching this book together think with the essay but change its shape. They practice something we could call immersive marginalia or even contrapuntal form. I think of this rhetorical intervention/invention as *witch stichomythia*. In tragic drama, *stichomythia* is a dialogic method where characters speak to each other in half lines, quickly, interrupting or completing thoughts, conveying urgency, displacement. Here, in stichomythic pieces, the archive and I (and others) speak across the page. We are separated by time and geography and death. We are connected through thought and grammar and form.

The communion of composition—writing with, which is a means of being with—can conjure, in de Certeau's phrase, "the relics of a walk through language." These relics are not just bones, not just objects, but become sonic subjects, felt presences that materially reverberate from tombs or hollows or digital archives to alter our understanding of how space can and does touch the body when, as Jean-Luc Nancy writes, "[t]he empty place of the absent [is] a place that is not empty." Throughout, I hope, the absent presence of the accused holds her space.

Such conjured conversations also commune with feminist rhetorical scholars such as Laura Micciche, who insists upon the disruptive potency of play, and Jacqueline Jones Royster and Gesa Kirsch, who invite work that is "dialogic, dialectical, reflective, reflexive, embodied, and anchored in an ethos of care, respect, and humility," and with early modern literary critics and historians such as Barbara Rosen, Deborah Willis, and Marion Gibson, who have rigorously interrogated the witch pamphlet genre, asking how ideas of "the witch" circulated in the Renaissance and beyond and thereby urging further response.

We walk with our relics through the woods of language (un)learned and looked for. The night is long, the paths unmarked. Nalo Hopkinson's narrator might remind us of this in "Riding the Red," a tale of what grandmothers try to teach their granddaughters, their daughers, and themselves before it's too late. I read Hopkinson's story alongside Sir Thomas More's *Utopia* and near my grandmother's death in late autumn (the other having died two springs before), as I read a 1587 chronicle of Joan Cason's trial and execution for invoking evil spirits and Scottish minister Robert Kirk's 17th-century notebook of fairy beliefs—charting not miniature frivolities but the burdens and possibilities of second sight. What's read takes strange shape in what's written—"a fabulative form of knowledge production," as Holly Pester writes. Put another way, in these woods the stichomythic bid for dialogue becomes co-walker, echo, trace, text message. There it is changed; there, given a chance, it changes.

[*A True & Just Record* comes from the title of a particularly virulent, violent, and manipulative pamphlet published in London during the English witch trials: *A true and iust Recorde, of the Information, Examination and Confession of all the Witches, taken at S. Oses in the countie of Essex: whereof some were executed, and other some entreated according to the determination of Lawe*, 1582. See also Marion Gibson's *Early Modern Witches: Witchcraft Cases in Contemporary Writing* and Barbara Rosen's *Witchcraft in England, 1558-1618*.

The book's epigraph is from the pamphlet *The Examination and Confession of certaine Wytches at Chensforde in the Countie of Essex, before the Quenes maiesties Judges, the xxvi. daye of July, ANNO. 1566*.

"Witch Stichomythia: Chances, Changes, & Strange Shapes" quotes Michel de Certeau's "The Unnamable," from *The Practice of Everyday Life*; "Distinct Oscillation" from Jean-Luc Nancy's *The Ground of the Image*; Jacqueline Jones Royster and Gesa Kirsch's *Feminist Rhetorical Practices*; Holly Pester's "Archive Fanfiction"; and *The Wonderfull yeare. 1603. Wherein is shewed the picture of London, lying sicke of the Plague*.]

Echo

I will not talk with thee
For thou art a dead thing

Thou art a dead thing

I will not talk with thee
I talk with thee

The intimate offices answer

Dead: state of being (art)   Dead: trace of creation (art)

Echo: A sound rebounding to a noise or voice in a valley or wood
A resounding or giving again of the voice

And where shall we meet? And when?

In the meantime a familiar or less
Familiar

Relic: some text, your shadow, this hour

[Near the conclusion of Scottish minister Robert Kirk's notebook of observations on fairy beliefs, compiled circa 1691 and published after his death, comes a section entitled: "An Exposition of the Difficult Words in the Foregoing Treatises." I borrow and quote at various points: "Echo: A sound rebounding to a noise or voice in a valley or wood; a resounding or giving again of the voice"; "Topical spirits: That haunt one place and not another"; and "Utopias: A nation invented by men's fancies." *The Secret Commonwealth: An Essay on the Nature and Actions of the Subterranean (and for the Most Part) Invisible People, heretofore Going under the Name of Elves, Fauns & Fairies.* "Echo" also quotes John Webster's play, *The Duchess of Malfi*, 1623.]

Upon Information, Belief

Imprimis, wonder appears each day wearing astonishing armaments.
Imprimis, how soon can we seek the intercessory?

Imprimis, the Office for the Dead works from home.
Imprimis, more difficult the Eucharist.

Imprimis, concerning form: of God, of execution, of poem.
Imprimis, form of rest. As in, did you sleep well? As in, eternal?

Imprimis, a painting of Mary & Jesus hosts the Three Living & the
Three Dead.
Imprimis, do you know the evening prayer for getting my kid to bed?

Imprimis, dreaming, the familiar turns crooked & unable to tell time.
Imprimis, a spirit is wise like that.

Imprimis, morning slips up: cunning, swollen, fast.
Imprimis, between us certain things are only spoken or they are
spoken only between us.

Imprimis, name *witch* the once-said.
Imprimis, wonder which to cast, which to keep.

Joan Cason: Executed for Invocation, 1586

Then was she carried back to their prison,
which they call the White house.

> Joan Cason, spelled Ione in the *Chronicles* called Holinshed's
> wherein her carriage is reported, held
> not guilty of bewitching Sara Cook's child—only
> a thought-lesser but not lessor-included offense.

And because there was no matter of inuocation
giuen in euidence against hir,

> *invocation*—neither object nor substance but exercise or practice
> the guilty of which we, unsummoned, call *practicer*
> (her jury exercising a *meant well*, a dare
> we say misspent kind of kindness?)—neither substantiated

nor proued in or by anie accusation, whereby
the iurie might haue anie colour to condemne hir

> for condemnation hangs on accusation the known neighbors'
> non-frivolous proof can sustain—*lay it in a hot fire*
> *the tile will sparkle and fly;*

therfore: hir execution was staied by the space
of three daies after judgement was giuen.

Given not a gift but a span, a length soon of rope
now of time meant to end time:
between, how far one might go.
Three mean days the interval between longed-for & dead.

In the meane time, she was persuaded
by sundrie preachers and learned men to confesse it.

Recommence the convincing, denials of which won't *quell*
the re-gathering, thundering storm. Persuasion
of the wind & its arraignments cry in the wall
Go to, go to, go to.

But no persuasion could preuaile, to make hir acknowledge
anie other criminall offense, but hir lewd life

—but these walls refuse to stay still
standing & we touch where, uninvited, judgment curls:
a life to acknowledge & to possess, hers?—

and adulterous conuersation with one Mason,
whose house she kept whilest he was in health,

not a discourse *honestly confessed*,
a practice *that he had the use of:*
the held, *her body,*
she was the beholden,

and whose person she tended whilest he was sicke;
with whome she was conuersant at the houre of his death,

making tending prepositional through the hour to
the very minute, minute & entire, in
a last entry, conversation & care, both versions of turning toward.
A preposition makes possible the turning away,

mainteining his concupiscence all the daies of his life;
and in the end abused the trust reposed in hir,

parallel furrows of (mis)deed planted:
what the body (*use of*) gives, misgives, what the body (*he had*) takes,
(im)practical mistakes

touching the disposition of certeine bequests,
which he made hir onelie priuie vnto.

Testamentary attestation as decreation: *I make thee*
sole executor, because I lov'de thee best.
If one has heirs one is
no longer.

For he died of the plague, for feare of which
infection none other durst repaire vnto him;

enfolded in the turn, another: inside the dying, fear;
prospect of pandemic contamination severs just *most*,
sends the other, marked *essential*,
unto: repair where connection cannot not be—

so as she vsed that matter
according to hir wicked conscience.

Matter confessed to misuse, no matter not for the use
convicted, so long as *wicked*, adjectival, attaches, archival,
the subject can be attached: miscarried
from unexecuted will to her place of execution.

[The left-sided text (to which line breaks have been added) comes from
Raphael Holinshed's *Chronicles of England, Scotland, and Ireland*, London,
1587. The right-sided text quotes or refers to H.D.'s *Trilogy: The Walls*
Do Not Fall, Tribute to the Angels, The Flowering of the Rod; Simone Weil's
Gravity and Grace; and Isabella Whitney's "The maner of her Wyll, and
what she left to London: and all those in it: at her departing," 1573.]

Story of Grandmother

Call this art of witchcraft an art
like the poem, paid for in blood,
milk, bread. Through the mouth all desires
known and willed into being, doing *as she was in structed*,
which means speaking the body of an old wives'
tale, the one where the witch

spun is a girl, twelve, spinning herself this claim: witch,
which is what opens the art
of want, the audacity to demand: sheep, wealth, wife,
a promise if she would *fyrste consent*. But spell love with blood,
and the bargained-for breaks down (learned
once desire's

been given into), her desires
said aloud and so allowed, briefly, to have what a witch
gets *delyuered her in the lykenesse of* a cat, her elder-taught
art, this art of domestic care, which is the art
of birthing to form what wasn't: sheep, wife, dead. The blood-
formed must be un-formed in the non-wife.

Here, a girl not taken to wife
after consummation of desire,
douting her self with childe pays blood
to waste his goodes, touch the wolf dead: witch
knowledge made a home economics, an essential art
home-schooled

on the sly: *take a certayne herbe and drinke it*. If they don't teach
you, if the courts bar you, go to the midwives or the old wives
with their familiars (not the unfamiliar who art
elsewhere desiring
another). Call the cunning woman, call the witch
called from your own self, homespun, let the unplanned bleed

out. Come, cat in a basket: drink this poem, drink this blood,
Little Red Cap holds a lesson
on endings. Years gulp days and the granddaughter witch
yet founde not the quietnes that she desyred in her life- or wife-
state: desire
came in a morninge the shape of the still—art,

feasted on. Desire baked blood-warm. Witch,
thicken through instruction the poet's first nurse-milk:
art is a cake from the oven eaten by an old wife.

[The italicized text of the sestina comes from the pamphlet *The Examination and confession of certaine Wytches at Chensforde in the Countie of
Essex*. Elizabeth Frauncis, who purportedly confessed that when she was
twelve her grandmother gave her a cat called Sathan that could grant her
wishes, is credited as saying that some fifteen or sixteen years later she
traded the cat for a cake. Elizabeth was not executed at this time, but is
presumed to be the Elizabeth Fraunces convicted of and executed for
witchcraft in 1579.]

Antique Incantation

As Horace tells it Canidia's love / Potion comes from young liver. The liver,
You say, is a beast. Caught in the quiver / Between sanguification source and trove:

Naughty, filtered treasures cull stores of / Steato, bad blood, blackouts but a sliver
Of the buried, how these humor rivers / Draw down to the bile dark sea. Love-

Meddling, don't forget, touches fear's heart. / Fear, that which makes us shiver, awake
To the fragile, ferocious, tender-fanged / Organ peddling death or the possessed hart.

All love charms stake political claims. / Invocations to gaze, to taste, to take.

"Utopias: A nation invented by men's fancies"

Be quiet. I'm working.

***

Sir Thomas More refused to swear
         an oath of allegiance to his king

      hoping silence could = consent.

***

What will happen when you find me purpled & pretty, a witch
in the woods—

      What when you conjure me in the tree, when you take a
      hand, ask if I want to
go—

   What if I do not say—

***

(I have made assumptions about the I,
   about the you,

about how to distinguish the oath from the elegy or—

> more troubling?—the hymn.)

***

A refusal to swear there argued
for each side—but execution can't cut 2 ways.

Roy Moore had 2.6 tons of 10 commandments in Alabama.

***

In the schoolyard mornings children would stand & offer—

> little birds in wooden words through so many
> mouths

the spell opened like one.

***

Too late a list of participants (incomplete)

I = girl no more
I = what does that mean a vaginal or age cutoff therefore
I = closed essentialized translation problem but in any event (still?)
  silent

you = king or king's men or capturing or captured forces or friends or
  wolf & why militant
you = maybe only always the reader & where does that leave us

***

Sir Thomas More coined *utopia*
Note: @ meals women sit *on the outside, so that if a woman has a sudden
  qualm or pain, such as occasionally happens during pregnancy, she may
  get up without disturbing the others and go off to the nurses.*

Note: Do Not Disturb

Quiet the girl sits in the cradle
of an oak quietly cradled—

What can she do? What can be done?

***

Once upon a time in the schoolyard learning to mouth more paths over

not yet knowing
of kneeling even

the mouths that don't move.

***

*I meant to tell my little girl . . . before she set off on her own, so pretty with
her little basket.* So goes the story.

***

Be quiet. I'm working.

[The foregoing quotes, in italics, Thomas More's *Utopia* and Nalo Hopkinson's "Riding the Red," *Skinfolk.*]

Joan of Arc:
Third Public Session,
February 24, 1431

1.

Never saw or never saw near
or never only as far as she knew?

Reporting acts of the quasi-collective one sometimes

joins (so sometimes doesn't) as branches
bedecked at times left, at times taken.

The pull of wandering aflame.

Time enters after: where
an after, so a before.

Dancing *when they were Fire*, perhaps. Singing, more.

What is called comes close enough
to the door, which is close enough

to ignite.

Enter another
fairy-tale teller

fixing the time: not nearby but at.

So she says,
she says no.

She will keep to herself
what she knows.

Go back to your foreknowledge, the forespoken a calling

forth of what would let being become
meant to be. Go, call on other springs.

Burn other trees.

2.

Asked about a certain tree near her village, she said that close by the village of Domrémy is a tree called the ladies' tree, and others call it the tree of the fairies, fées *in French, which is near a spring. She heard that those sick with the fever drink from the spring, and they go in search of its water for healing. She saw this herself, but she does not know whether they are cured. . . . She said that sometimes she went for a walk with the other girls and made wreaths near the tree for the image of the Blessed Mary of Domrémy.*

3.

Topical Spirits: That haunt one place and not another.

4.

Sick, they drink. This is the order of desire.

What can be seen: seeking.
What cannot:

In search of needs a burning to go from.

The fairy tree Spenser will call *warlike*, in May
makes beauty thronged by demand,

belonging by custom not
by calling nor by name.

Is a walk with girls proximate

to the walk of the sick and which is other? Wreaths
left nearby for the nearby image of one blessed

and one blessing

the near enough to hear, far enough to split
sickness, girlhood. Said fringe of fairy belief.

She hears too from those so-called of bodies

politic and church, having seen the there-gathered.
But what's said is stuck at proving

a statement made, not any other truth.

["Joan of Arc: Third Public Session, February 24, 1431" quotes testimony from Joan of Arc's "preparatory trial." The poem also quotes or refers to *Emily Dickinson: The Gorgeous Nothings*, a collection of facsimile reproductions of Dickinson's manuscript envelope poems; Michel de Certeau's "Spatial Stories," from *The Practice of Everyday Life*; and Edmund Spenser's *The Faerie Queene* (1590), especially the list of trees in the Wandering Wood, the site of Errour's Den (Book I, canto i).]

Topical Spirits

Daughters, hold fast to find your dwelling / Which I should pluralize and so prepare
For you to be other than always paired / Visions seen inside of this propelling

Moment where day turns to year, compelling / Momentum otherward. You yell *unfair!*
How dare you! to dispel the erstwhile lares / From their settled stares (*hold, mercy*), foretelling

Via lactation or location haunts / One's absence cannot not countermand
And complicate, your glares neither an hour's / Opposite nor our only assurance. Power

Clocks its ways: so fixate, re-enchant, demand / To share in the provisions of wonder.

Tales for Children

To share with the specters your collected wants— / Two sisters, a thimble, a pestle, bread,
The blood of your grandmother, her bones, dead / Fingers ironing italic-serifed fonts—

Carry your cap, cape, and basket against gaunt / Wolves. Pocket teeth, kerchiefs of cakes fed
The dogs and the dying, skin to burn or shed, / Combs, rings, nettles, coins—to offer,

Not to flaunt. Every path asks for payment. / So you must needs parcel and open
The spaces that write the songs you carry / The guts the vessels the heartsick you carry.

Even your ghosts give directives: Keep me close. / Lament. Stitch milk and stars in this raiment.

Elizabeth Fraunces:
Executed for Witchcraft,
April 1579

Imprimis, the saied Elizabeth Fraunces cõfessed
that about Lent last (as she now remembreth)

> —past events presently recollected become the confessional
> said-made-true, a month after Easter,
> read on this the Sixth Sunday of the same—

she came to one Pooles wife her neighbour,
and required some olde yest of her,

> encounter with, which is exposure to, the other
> already ordered by possession—old, common,
> circle compressed to its least needs.
> Without it? A passing over,

but beyng denied the same, she departed towardes one good wife
Osbornes house a neighbour dwelling thereby of whome she had yest,

> denied: pivot, departure marks the away
> from & the towards & in the towards, there might victory
> dwell. Herein, *the precarious finitude of being*, herein
> having long-since entered, geometry

and in her waie going towardes the saied
goodwife Osbornes house, shee cursed Pooles wife,

from the departing vector turned hers, curse
the other, curse her, curse you—hurry!
a curse carries momentum—

and badde a mischief to light uppon her,
for that she would giue her no yest,

for Poole's wife's inhospitable not-giving,
for her neighborly failure unequal to the task
of circular fulfillment, for that.

Whereuppon sodenly in the waie she hard a greate noise,
and presently there appered unto her

an apparition, come in the instant you can't catch, only
adverbially—*sodenly, presently*—outline as auditory.
First, noise. The curse is the *third man*
or demon [that] cries out between us,

a Spirite of a white colour in seemyng like to a little rugged Dogge,
standyng neere her uppon the grounde,

enter spirit, shaggy-small, fairy-tale helper
angling from apparition (shade of, ghost
of) to the close, the real: here upon the ground

who asked her whether she went?
shee aunswered for suche thinges as she wanted,

spirit-dog speaking from the ground up, passage
naming passage, vectored. Do you go & to where?
I go to what I lack. This is
the geometry of history,

and she tolde him therewith that she could
gette no yeest of Pooles wife

in body departing from refusal of that which
would inflate, create, bubble-round exhalation fermented
by the telling

and therefore willed the same Spirite to goe to her and plague her,
which the Spirite promised to doe,

in spirit back-facing, facing refusal—*a logic*
of willing & desiring weaponized?—
will the spirit

but first he bad her giue him somewhat,

because nothing is free.
Consider this: where the going & the coming cross—exchange,
H.D.'s *geometry of perfection*—

then she hauing in her hand a crust of white bread,
did bite a peece thereof and threwe it uppon the grounde,

yeast-made, hand-held, through the body given.
Consider this: no exploration's antecedent, a promise
secured through bread's *proof & rest,*

which she thinketh he tooke up and so went his waie,
but before he departed from her she willed hym

from the landing what matter is
taken up can be sent—from her
through him to her

too plague Pooles wife in the head,

to hurt the heart of where refusal lies, hurt
how the said emerges, hurt *the locus of need*. Plague what cannot be
assuaged

and since then she neuer sawe him,
but she hath harde by her neighbours

of a spirit gossiped into invisible,
what slant record remains we call memory & rumor, injury
fresh-brewed in the (re)hearing

that the same Pooles wife was greuously pained in her head
not longe after, and remayneth very sore payned still,

because the vector is an arrow sent back the direction one
comes empty from, between the two
the triangle of the demon third, an acute hurt

for on saturdaie last past this Examinate talked with her.

Lent last, Saturday last—
talking like this is ordinary time, reading like it's past.

.

[The left-sided text (line breaks added) comes from the pamphlet *A Detection of damnable driftes, practized by three Witches arraigned at Chelmisforde in Essex, at the laste Assises there holden, whiche were executed in Aprill. 1579*. The right-sided text quotes or refers to H.D.'s *Trilogy*; Louis Marin's *Food for Thought*; Michel Serres' *Rome: The First Book of Foundations* and *Geometry: The Third Book of Foundations*; and Julian Yates' *Of Sheep, Oranges, and Yeast: A Multispecies Impression.*]

Having Fallen Alone at Home

Pulse of regret, reserved. / Here, conserve what you know about healing
The heart-sore when older pains come stealing / Into reckoning the once-done. Observe:

Here, a touch and the shroud goes down. Nerves / Curved hot to the hip like proof sealing
Up a past. How one step—bent—sent you reeling / Feeling near 98 revolutions swerve.

Tilt your forearms at the ground but the ground / Will not give or forgive or consider
How far there is to go if there's no gate / Back to an Eden where the evening sounds

Were heartbeat, shuffled sheets, sirens the weight / Of whose summons grew faint, grew fainter.

Boundary Stones

She said *A good childe howe art thou loden:*
And so went thrice out of the doors

We watched the going out the coming in
A good childe howe art thou loden

We watched each close open
The apparition repetition sings forth

Tell me *good woman thou art not loden:*
And go to unburdened out of the doors

[The first two lines of the triolet borrow from *A true and iust Recorde*, 1582. In the pamphlet, Grace Thurlowe describes an attempted healing spell by cunning woman turned accused witch Ursley Kempe. Ursley was later convicted and executed.]

Elizabeth Sawyer: Executed for Witchcraft on Thursday, April 19, 1621

A Great, and long suspition was held
of this person to be a witch, and the eye

> holds its great and long gaze reading that which
> would not be seen, which
> is not the same as not being,

of Mr. Arthur Robinson, a worthy Iustice
of Peace, who dweleth at Totnam neere to her,

> name-position-domicile clausally
> established, the circles of exclusion purple out. Classify
> who dwells near, who not. Dare we say we were or I

was watchfull ouer her, and her wayes,
and that not without iust cause;

> not just the subject (body) but the subject's (body's)
> movements, severable or several, will demystify the dogged
> object of justice

stil hauing his former long suspition of her,
by the information of her neighbours

—suspicion, his; neighbors, hers; information,
the multiple. The multiple *hardens*
around the unity of the corpse

that dwelt about her: from suspitiõ,
to proceed to great presumptions,

pregnant the held dwells
great with

seeing the death of Nurse-children and Cattell,
strangely and suddenly to happen.

Seeing the deaths of sudden
milk economies, accusation (barking! barking!) incorporates
to make the mourning-
born incarnate.

And to finde out who should bee the author
of this mischiefe, an old and ridiculous

reader, how we read with suspicions
even as we *suckle at these multiple*
and old breasts, sources of our cultural formations,
for such are our methods, for such

custome was vsed, which was to plucke
the Thatch of her house, and to burne it,

burn the plucked piece of her
house becomes strip her body to nipples moles veins privies hitherto hidden
(here lies
the multiple's metonymic threat)

and it being so burnd, the author of such
mischiefe should presently then come:

burned-thatch-turned-inverted-hearth-without-
respite toward which comes the author we see
uncalled for: call her witch

and it was obserued and affirmed to the Court,
that Elizabeth Sawyer would presently frequent

> at the door the threshold for stumbling on whereupon
> the seen becomes said becomes act. Offer
> into evidence presence as proof,

the house of them that burnt the thatch
which they pluckt of her house, and come

> now our uninvited guest, sole object of the multiple summoned
> by burning the by-extension her, which
> is not the same as wanted, which
> is the same as wanting,

without any sending for.

[The left-sided text (line breaks added) comes from the pamphlet *The wonderfull discouerie of Elizabeth Sawyer, a Witch, late of Edmonton, her conuiction and condemnation and Death*, written by Newgate prison chaplain Henry Goodcole, 1621. The right-sided text quotes or refers to Michel Serres' *Rome* and *Statues: The Second Book of Foundations* and Eve Kosofsky Sedgwick's "Paranoid Reading and Reparative Reading, or, You're So Paranoid, You Probably Think This Essay Is About You" in *Touching Feeling: Affect, Pedagogy, Performativity*. Elizabeth's story is the basis for the domestic tragedy (and self-proclaimed tragicomedy) *The Witch of Edmonton* by William Rowley, Thomas Dekker, and John Ford (1621).]

Can You See the Milky Way Where You Are?

Lament milk. Stitch stars for the dead's raiment. / For the living, same. Lament what short view
Can't liken breath and no breath beneath the yews. / Stitch milk. Drop stars in your pocket. Lament.

The dead with their star-eyes and stone raiment / Shape boundaries of the nonliving you
Won't see, not with these eyes or this view. / Milk-satin's silent. So's a star's lament.

Stars are the dead caught alive and milk-shiny. / Sip stellar parallax via teeninsy
Lenses and that which burns will go on burning. / *Such work it takes to age!* Learning, unlearning,

The dust of the once. Fold up and stow / For later those maps the thirsty might follow.

Kate Bolton Bonnici   45

"[C]ontrol the moon, make flows and ebbs"

Forlorn, those maps the thirsty might follow. / For now: where the river curved, it curves still
At the noontide night's dismantling will / Misremember, an accident of hollow-

Stalked saints. Fortune has this habit: swallow / Household complicities, blood-threshed, fill
To spilling sibylline footprints until / We swill the overflow. Solemn, Apollo

Gives no guide here, Mercury no legend / For distilling the past or other plots.
Even as the waters rise, we tarry. / Early, emboli break from a common clot.

Each break begins an ending destined / For revelation: keep your coin for the ferry.

[The title quotes Prospero in Shakespeare's *The Tempest*. Prospero describes the powers of the absent witch Sycorax.]

"[T]hose whom the flood carries are the buried"

Remember to keep your coin for the ferry / In your purse or mouth, not lost like my mother
Lost her hairdresser's fare in the other / Hand. Six and sob-soaked, what she'd meant to carry

How her mother told her to gone as fairy / Gold. Going to and from school my grandmother
Caught the river ferry with her brother. / Will she be carried from the cemetery?

We rode the ferry across Mobile Bay, / Both dock points christened for Civil War forts,
One of which had stone steps we called *Blood Stained* / Knowing nothing. Delta waterways

(Names: fey payment for theft) as before sort / Scuttled bones, the vessels for taken remains.

[The title comes from Virgil's *Aeneid*. The Mobile Bay Ferry travels between Fort Morgan and Fort Gaines. Chickasaw Creek and the Tombigbee, Alabama, Mobile, Tensaw, and Apalachee Rivers flowing into the Mobile-Tensaw Delta are some of the waterways named for the peoples and languages indigenous to the lands that became the states of Alabama and Florida.]

Elder | Ledger

And they say:

> *She was a very old woman, about the*
> *age of*

you, 17 years ago. Can you tick

back

> *Fourescore yeares,*

and what if you were

> *and had been a Witch for*

as long as you lived in that house, 14+

> *fiftie yeares. She dwelt in the Forrest*
> *of Pendle,*

and you by the park
of pines. Hers,

> *a vaste place,*

near Fence. Your fence flattened
from tempests

> *fitte for her profession:*

which also meant teaching.

> *What shee committed in her time, no*
> *man knowes.*

This is surely true.
This is always true.

> *Thus lived shee*
> *securely*

(thus indicate adverbs uncertainty)

> *for many yeares, brought up*

—same as you were brought up?
same as you did the bringing up of?—

her owne Children,
instructed her Graund-children,

you managed a daughter's kids,

and took great care and paines to
bring them to be

capable in the general sense, as

able as

Witches. Shee was a generall agent
for the Deuill in all thefe partes:

of the whole familial
composition wherein we knew
of a without, where

no man escaped her, or her Furies,

sharpening,

that ever gave

instruction, inviolable until we took

from

them any occasion of offence, or
denyed them any

occasion of wanting such

thing they stood need of:

flip side, being denied the need

to offer.

And certaine it is, no man

nor woman nor child

neere them, was secure or free from

debt or

danger.

[The text on the right side of "Elder | Ledger" comes from *The Wonder-full Discoverie of Witches in the Countie of Lancaster. With the Arraignement and Triall of Nineteene notorious Witches, at the Assizes and generall Gaole deliverie, holden at the Castle of Lancaster, upon Munday, the seventeenth of August last, 1612*, by Thomas Potts. The quoted portion describes Elizabeth Southerns, also called "Old Demdike." According to the pamphlet, she "died in the Castle at *Lancaster* before she came to receiue her tryall."]

"The Wonderfull yeare.
1603"

when that which will kill is a *child named Sicknesse*
whom Death needs take upon him to nurse, and did so

droplets droplets

call it milk or other & what of the mother *droplets* after travail
disappeared

alone & 97 you try to row the *Stygian Ferry*

with a laptop

today we FaceTimed
your face aslant against

inner creases of a lampshade uncovering frustration
with the devices kids use

The Wonderfull yeare is a pamphlet of princes & plague

all the ways one can be
worm-written written in blackletter (font & as to the law—what is)

how some come from the maw of disease & others—

I will ask one of the schoolchildren to come
help me you say

knowing you
cannot

not in the time of virus

The Wonderfull yeare lends a queen's funeral to a nation of tears
I now read: *droplets droplets*

tears not saliva
nor snot not yet

a queen's last resolve resolutely becoming pandemonium

absent resolution a pandemic absence

stare at the screen it blinks communion stare at the screen it lets in
breeze & on the breeze

droplets

cover the faces of the dead
& the living

quiet five coffins sans mourners
where do we go with no lament?

The Wonderfull yeare begins in March

one called a prince died March 24   (*mirabilis annus*)
one called a pope spoke March 27   (*urbi et orbi*)

Francis walks across St. Peter's Square where the rains fell

what we cannot cross: state lines county lines
home lines here

how we have one—rooms & hallway & roof

droplets droplets a slow step & a slow step no umbrella &
the raindrops fell

lean on a monsignor up the steps no railing lean step lean
where the rains fell & keep falling

a storm a sleeping god a startled & a scared many, dread

filled *such an houre is in utterable: let us goe further*

in Ovid, plague is a *murrain* that *raves*
& you call to say you can recover

the home page should you find
(*in this Mare mortuum*) you're lost

murrain is a word I don't know like you don't know
how to scroll down

The Wonderfull yeare turns to April: time's cruelest signpost

the daughter in my lap howls louder than when isolation's frustration

won't drop
lets her tears mix up lonely with pissed

I know this night *spirites walke* & infection's gone winged

I wonder if you are
I resolve you are

not yet

"Then the liars and the swearers are fools"

Illuminating what commands stir / Against good reason this consummate
Error of subject, address, or estimate. / When you, sweet prattler, ask: *what's a traitor?*

The answer is not: you do as birds / Do with what you hold or what you get
If you don't fear the lime and clear the net. / *Little wren, how will you live?* Not set for,

Reading: market, virus, coup d'état signs. / Not set for, watching; flagstaff hilts tilt
To keep the charms wound up. This time: guilt / Unequivocal, bound up with worms and flies

Enough I swear we'll hence how the messenger / Says to. It's too late for a messenger.

[Some phrases above come from Shakespeare's *Macbeth*. The title quotes
Lady Macduff's son in conversation with her before their deaths.]

Love Charms

1.

To speak is to open
An invitation to wounding.
Silence, we know.

2.

While Demeter mourned
She forbade speech, nightly
Nursed another by fire.

3.

Mark a mystery of
Love: love's return.

4.

Hard dark, and the moon
Hones the slow blade, one body
At the very verge of light.

[The phrase "very verge of light" comes from Virgil's *Georgics*. In her book *At the Bottom of the Garden*, Diane Purkiss describes the prohibition on speaking about fairy encounters: "Revelation is danger. The closed mouth is a safe mouth. Any opening of the body is fatal."]

Pronouncement beside a Red Recliner

You were the first in all history
To say: *she died, she died, she died*

Death: this open-mouthed mystery
You were the first in all history

To shape the nothing her story
Becomes: lovely-dumb, tongue-tied

Your burden: enter into history
To say she died: she died: she died

[The triolet, with some modification, quotes H.D.'s *Helen in Egypt* and Gerard Manley Hopkins' "Habit of Perfection."]

Elizabeth Stile: Executed for Witchcraft, 1579

Also this is not to be forgotten,
that the said Mother Stile,

> still, reader, remember the said and picture her
> no longer one more but a lone life, alone even.

> > *Even in the course of our life*
> > *the vortex of the origin remains present*

> preserving through inclination how the singular
> self or body comes to the fore as a bright being,

beeyng at the tyme of her apprehension,
so well in healthe of bodie and limmes,

> limned by shadows, molecular chains not wearing
> forgetting until touched, in-breaths, swearing still

> > *until the end and silently accompanies*
> > *our existence at every moment.*

> Momentous old mother, stride, out-bounding,
> cover ground like seven-league boots, like that,

that she was able, and did goe on foote,
from Windsor vnto Readyng vnto the Gaile,

this jail, the gaoler's grail (iambic thus drunk
from), if not now then, yes, at another time.

At times it gets closer; at other
times it distances itself

from healing: a hell's helix—why confession when
communion clicks one turn from need to known,

whiche are twelue miles
distaunt.

Too far to touch or taste these travailed miles,
too far to hear what's coming, to see so much,

so much that we are no longer
able to glimpse it

(in-between: turned milk, village untwinings,
solar storms radiating, palpable and unread).

Shortly after that she had made
the aforesaied confession, the other Witches

elsewhere accused of sending dogs, toads.
If one sends bees, one wonders how to see

or to perceive its hushed swarming.
But, at decisive moments, it seizes us

through seizure or trance or dreamspeak, or our
wanting mouths were seized or our seizing wants

were apprehended, and were brought
to the said Gaile, the said Mother Deuell

(the said-devil brought back to mother
form, which remains our present origin

and drags us inside it;
we then suddenly realize that we are

not alone still turning and we long only to be
still again or to forget what our longings did)

did so bewitche her and others
(as she confessed vnto the Iailer)

as she wished unto the confessor, can you assemble
bits, pieces, what's become of these our portions?—

ourselves nothing other than a fragment
of the beginning that continues to spin

the threads we tell I imagine
red, raveling, blood-withered

with her Enchauntmentes, that the vse of all
her limmes and senses, were taken quite

quiet. How to hear the last breath?
How to care without a final curing

in the whirlpool from which
our life derives,

desire, derivative, drawn late and lonely, desire
the been-widowed, age-scratched, alms-bound:

from her, and her Toes did rotte of her feete,
and she was laied vppon a Barrowe,

barren or barely outlasting what turbulence
comes from *crowd*, from *commotion—full* too,

to swirl in it until
it reaches the point of infinite

>   (which is not a point and which crumbles under
>   these crowds) crowing, the body's failing limit

as a moste vglie creature to beholde,
and so brought before the Iudges,

>   once book then door, the threshold is not absence
>   but a before-presence, there at the missing, builds

>   *negative pressure*
>   *and disappears—*

[The left-sided text (line breaks added) comes from the pamphlet *A Rehearsall both straung and true, of hainous and horrible actes committed by Elizabeth Stile, Alias Rockingham, Mother Dutten, Mother Deuell, Mother Margaret, Fower notorious Witches, apprehended at winsore in the Countie of Barks. and at Abbington arraigned, condemned, and executed, on the 26 daye of Februarie laste Anno. 1579*. The right-sided text, with line breaks also added, comes from Giorgio Agamben's *The Fire and the Tale*. The center words are mine.]

Care Does Not Measure All Forms of Rest

Respite, we'll call our masque. Our quiet task / Performed as holding, as offering outward
Through sign or palm uncovered toward / Another, this other. Beloved, I bask

In your being as wine drunk with milk. I ask: / Let the line of your hand that breaks break forward
At the line in mine own rivening and scored / Bifurcations some futures may unmask.

Quiet marks the crenulation of skin / At your wrist: composed, not quite closed, preserve
Of standard histories in foliation, / These made-unmade striations, variations

Of loop-to-flow, laminar-tangled print. / Press here your pulse without regret or reserve.

The Last Story Grandmother Told Me

We were never scared, playing
Each day among the graves.

Read the headstones, we knew
How we knew: *sing the names*.

Bibliography

Pamphlets in order of appearance:

A true and iust Recorde, of the Information, Examination and Confession of all the Witches, taken at S. Oses in the countie of Essex: whereof some were executed, and other some entreated according to the determination of Lawe, 1582, *Early English Books Online (EEBO)*.

The Examination and Confession of certaine Wytches at Chensforde in the Countie of Essex, before the Quenes maiesties Judges, the xxvi. daye of July, Anno. 1566, EEBO.

A Detection of damnable driftes, practized by three Witches arraigned at Chelmisforde in Essex, at the laste Assises there holden, whiche were executed in Aprill. 1579, EEBO.

The wonderfull discouerie of Elizabeth Sawyer, a Witch, late of Edmonton, her conuiction and condemnation and Death, by Henry Goodcole, 1621, *EEBO*.

The Wonderfull Discoverie of Witches in the Countie of Lancaster. With the Arraignement and Triall of Nineteene notorious Witches, at the Assizes and generall Gaole deliverie, holden at the Castle of Lancaster, upon Munday, the seventeenth of August last, 1612, by Thomas Potts, *EEBO*.

The Wonderfull yeare. 1603. Wherein is shewed the picture of London, lying sicke of the Plague, EEBO.

A Rehearsall both straung and true, of hainous and horrible actes committed by Elizabeth Stile, Alias Rockingham, Mother Dutten, Mother Deuell, Mother Margaret, Fower notorious Witches, apprehended at winsore in the Countie of Barks. and at Abbington arraigned, condemned, and executed, on the 26 daye of Februarie laste Anno. 1579, EEBO.

Other references:

Agamben, Giorgio. *The Fire and the Tale*. Translated by Lorenzo Chiesa, Stanford University Press, 2017.

Bervin, Jan and Marta Werner, editors. *Emily Dickinson: The Gorgeous Nothings*. New Directions, 2013.

De Certeau, Michel. *The Practice of Everyday Life*. Translated by Steven F. Rendall, University of California Press, 1984.

Dolan, Frances E. *Dangerous Familiars: Representations of Domestic Crime in England, 1550-1700*. Cornell University Press, 1994.

Enoch, Jessica, Danielle Griffin, and Karen Nelson, editors. *Feminist Circulations: Rhetorical Explorations across Space and Time*. Parlor Press, 2022.

Gibson, Marion. *Reading Witchcraft: Stories of Early English Witches*. Routledge, 1999.

—. *Early Modern Witches: Witchcraft Cases in Contemporary Writing*. Routledge, 2000.

H.D. *Trilogy: The Walls Do Not Fall, Tribute to the Angels, The Flowering of the Rod*. Edited by Aliki Barnstone, New Directions, 1998 (first published 1946).

—. *Helen in Egypt*. New Directions, 1961.

Hobbins, Daniel, editor and translator. *The Trial of Joan of Arc*. Harvard University Press, 2005.

Holinshed, Raphael. *Chronicles of England, Scotland, and Ireland*, London, 1587 (1808 ed., IV, 891-893).

Hopkins, Gerard Manley. *Poems and Prose*. Edited by W.H. Gardner, Penguin, 1953.

Hopkinson, Nalo. "Riding the Red," *Skinfolk*. Warner Books, 2001.

Kirk, Robert. *The Secret Commonwealth: An Essay on the Nature and Actions of the Subterranean (and for the Most Part) Invisible People, heretofore Going under the Name of Elves, Fauns & Fairies*. Edited by Marina Warner, New York Review of Books, 2007.

Levack, Brian P. *The Witchcraft Sourcebook*. Routledge, 2015.

Marin, Louis. *Food for Thought*. Translated by Mett Hjort, Johns Hopkins University Press, 1997.

Miccicche, Laura. "Writing as Feminist Rhetorical Theory," in *Rhetorica in Motion: Feminist Rhetorical Methods & Methodologies*. Edited by Eileen E. Schell and K.J. Rawson, University of Pittsburgh Press, 2010.

More, Thomas. *Utopia*. Edited by George M. Logan and Robert M. Adams, Norton, 2011.

Nancy, Jean-Luc. *The Ground of the Image*. Translated by Jeff Fort, Fordham University Press, 2005.

Ovid. *Metamorphoses*. Translated by Arthur Golding and published in 1567. Edited by Madeleine Forey, Penguin Books, 2002.

Pester, Holly. "Archive Fanfiction: Experimental Archive Research Methodologies and Feminist Epistemological Tactics," *Feminist Review* 115, 2017.

Purkiss, Diane. *At the Bottom of the Garden: A Dark History of Fairies, Hobgoblins, and other Troublesome Things*. New York University Press, 2000.

Rosen, Barbara. *Witchcraft in England, 1558-1618*. University of Massachusetts Press, 1991.

Rowley, William, Thomas Dekker, and John Ford. *The Witch of Edmonton* (1621). Edited by Peter Corbin and Douglas Sedge in *Three Jacobean Witchcraft Plays*, Manchester University Press, 1989.

Royster, Jacqueline Jones and Gesa E. Kirsch. *Feminist Rhetorical Practices: New Horizons for Rhetoric, Composition, and Literacy Studies*. Southern Illinois University Press, 2012.

Sedgwick, Eve Kosofsky. "Paranoid Reading and Reparative Reading, or, You're So Paranoid, You Probably Think This Essay Is About You" in *Touching Feeling: Affect, Pedagogy, Performativity*, Duke University Press, 2002.

Serres, Michel. *Rome: The First Book of Foundations*. Translated by Randolph Burks, Bloomsbury, 2015.

—. *Statues: The Second Book of Foundations*. Translated by Randolph Burks, Bloomsbury, 2015.

—. *Geometry: The Third Book of Foundations*. Translated by Randolph Burks, Bloomsbury, 2017.

Shakespeare, William. *Macbeth*. Edited by William C. Carroll, Bedford/St. Martin's, 1999.

—. *The Tempest*. Edited by Virginia Mason Vaughan and Alden T. Vaughan, Arden Shakespeare, 2011.

Sharpe, James. *Instruments of Darkness: Witchcraft in Early Modern England*. University of Pennsylvania Press, 1996.

Spenser, Edmund. *The Faerie Queene* (1590). Edited by A.C. Hamilton, Routledge, 2013.

Virgil. *Georgics*. Translated by H.R. Fairclough and G.P. Goold, Harvard University Press, 1999.

—. *Aeneid*. Translated by H.R. Fairclough and G.P. Goold, Harvard University Press, 1999.

Webster, John. *The Duchess of Malfi* (1623). Edited by Michael Neill, Norton, 2015.

Weil, Simone. *Gravity and Grace*. Routledge, 2002.

Whitney, Isabella. "The maner of her Wyll, and what she left to London: and all those in it: at her departing," published 1573 and reprinted in *Isabella Whitney, Mary Sidney, and Aemilia Lanyer: Renaissance Women Poets*. Edited by Danielle Clark, Penguin, 2000.

Wilby, Emma. *Cunning Folk and Familiar Spirits: Shamanistic Visionary Traditions in Early Modern British Witchcraft and Magic*. Sussex Academic Press, 2013.

Willis, Deborah. *Malevolent Nurture: Witch-Hunting and Maternal Power in Early Modern England*, Cornell University Press, 1995.

Yates, Julian. *Of Sheep, Oranges, and Yeast: A Multispecies Impression*, University of Minnesota Press, 2017.

Acknowledgments

Grateful acknowledgment is made to the following journals for publication of these works, sometimes in different form: "Echo," "Joan Cason, Executed for Invocation, 1586," "Utopias: A nation invented by men's fancies," and "The Wonderfull yeare. 1603," *Foundry*; "Elizabeth Fraunces, Executed in April, 1579," *CounterText*; "Elizabeth Stile: Executed in 1579," *Synapsis*; "The Last Story Grandmother Told Me," *Dusie*; and "Story of Grandmother," *The Maine Review*. The sonnets are part of a larger sequence called "Via Lactea" in the Winter 2022 issue of *The Georgia Review*.

My warmest thanks to Simon Palfrey and Katharine Craik for believing that criticism can be literary and for creating a press that gives such criticism a tangible form in the world. Thank you for your wise and generous counsel. Thank you, as well, to Nathan Hamilton, James Hatton, Louise Aspinall, and everyone at Boiler House Press for supporting this book and for making it beautiful.

My immense gratitude to the Renaissance Project.

My absolute adoration of and affection for Julia Lee, Katie Ford, Heidi Brayman, Lowell Gallagher, Chris Chism, Arthur Little, Fred D'Aguiar, Annie Finch, and Barbara Fuchs. Thank you for reading and writing and encouraging and then for reading and writing and listening and encouraging even more—and for your friendship throughout.

Thank you, Deborah Willis, for welcoming me into your wonderful graduate seminar on the English witch trials.

To my family, love beyond measure. I am daily grateful to those here and for those who have gone on: Dan, Charlotte, Annie, Dad, Mom, Kathy, Will, Ali, Addie, Charlie, Lulu, Jeb, Anna, Calvin, Patricia, David, Meredith, Polly, Marie, Jeff, Clare, John, Jack, and Kath.

Bebe and GG, my matriarchs, this book is for you.

A True & Just Record
By Kate Bolton Bonnici

First published in this edition by Boiler House Press, 2023
Part of UEA Publishing Project
A True & Just Record copyright © Kate Bolton Bonnici

Author photograph by Ariella Maman

Editorial Coordination and Proofreading by James Hatton

Cover Design and Typesetting by Louise Aspinall
Typeset in Arnhem Pro

ISBN: 978-1-915812-17-9

Printed in the USA
CPSIA information can be obtained
at www.ICGtesting.com
JSHW072130191223
53999JS00017B/175